PLAY WITH
paper

Sara Lynn & Diane James

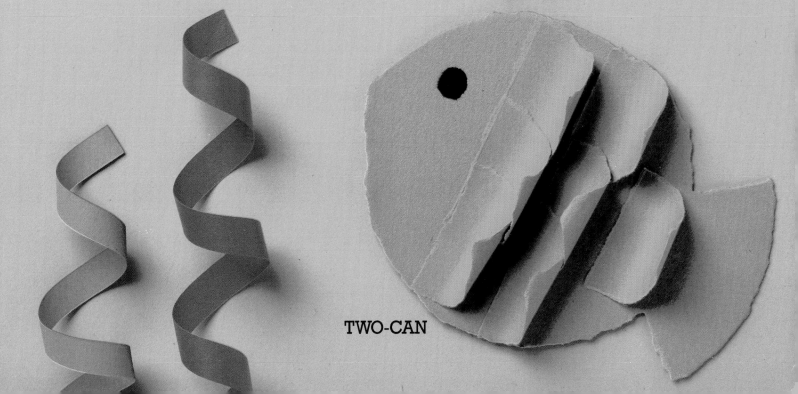

TWO-CAN

➋ Paper Play

Here are some ideas for using paper in different ways. You can use these suggestions for making a collage, for cards, for decorations and lots more! Try using all sorts of paper.

Crumpled Paper

Crumple a piece of paper in your hands. Flatten it out again. Look at the shape it makes.

Paper Curls

Ask a grown-up to cut some long strips of paper. Wind a strip round a thick knitting needle or pencil. Be very careful of the sharp points. Hold the end of the strip and gently pull it off the needle to make a paper curl! You could use paper curls to make party decorations.

Torn Paper

When you cut paper with scissors it has a straight edge. Try tearing paper into shapes. The edges will be rough. Make a collection of lots of different shapes of torn paper. Sort them into separate piles and use them to build up a picture.

➍ Fun Fish

These colourful fish are easy to make and you can use lots of different methods for decorating them. Look at some of the ideas on the next page.

Try using all sorts of different papers – brown paper, newspaper, paper napkins, old wrapping paper and tissue paper.

Ask a grown-up to help you cut some fish shapes from thin card.

Cut out pieces of coloured paper slightly larger than your fish shapes. Glue a piece of paper to one of the fish. Carefully tear the paper round the edge of the card.

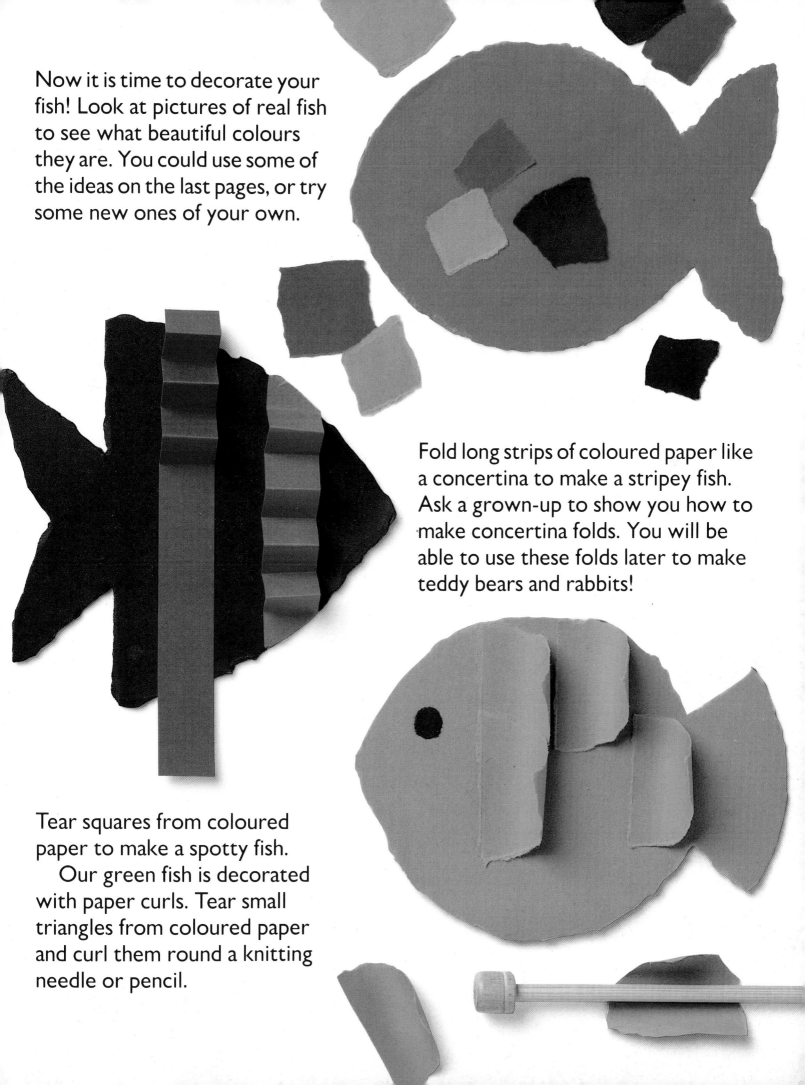

Now it is time to decorate your fish! Look at pictures of real fish to see what beautiful colours they are. You could use some of the ideas on the last pages, or try some new ones of your own.

Fold long strips of coloured paper like a concertina to make a stripey fish. Ask a grown-up to show you how to make concertina folds. You will be able to use these folds later to make teddy bears and rabbits!

Tear squares from coloured paper to make a spotty fish.
    Our green fish is decorated with paper curls. Tear small triangles from coloured paper and curl them round a knitting needle or pencil.

These brightly coloured fans will keep you cool on hot days. Take a rectangle of paper and make concertina folds like the ones on the previous page.

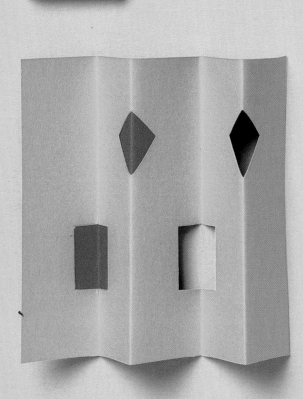

Decorate your fan by cutting shapes into the folds. Pinch the fan at one end and make a hole through all the thicknesses. Thread some string through and knot it.

Paper Beads

Ask a grown-up to cut some long
strips of paper, or use those sold to
make paper-chains. Roll a strip round
the handle of a wooden spoon.
Put a dab of glue on the end and
stick it down.

Another way to make paper beads is
to start with a long, thin triangle. Two
pieces of paper stuck together will
make a stronger bead! Starting with
the wide end, wind the triangle round
a thick pencil and stick the end down.
Thread the beads on shoelaces or
thin cord.

⑫ Animal Masks

Pretend to be a giant, cuddly bear! Glue some pale brown paper on to thin card. Ask a grown-up to trace round the bear's head to make a paper pattern. Tape the pattern to the card and cut round it. Cut out two holes for the eyes. Cut out ears and a nose from coloured paper and stick them down.

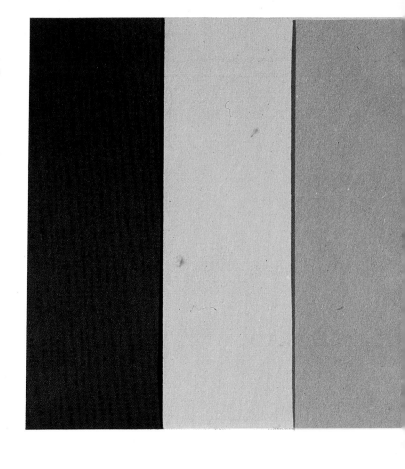

Ask a grown-up to make small holes on either side of the mask and thread some elastic through. Make a knot at the ends of the elastic to stop it slipping through. You will find some more ideas for making animal masks on the next two pages.

What other bear masks can you make?
How about a panda or a polar bear!

The next time you have a party, ask all
your friends to come as animals!

What other sorts of masks could you make? Try making a monster mask!

⑯ Bunch of Flowers

This beautiful bunch of flowers is made from paper napkins! When you take a napkin out of its packet it will be folded in four. Fold it in half to make a triangle. The folded edges should be together and the cut edges on the top. Fold the triangle again.

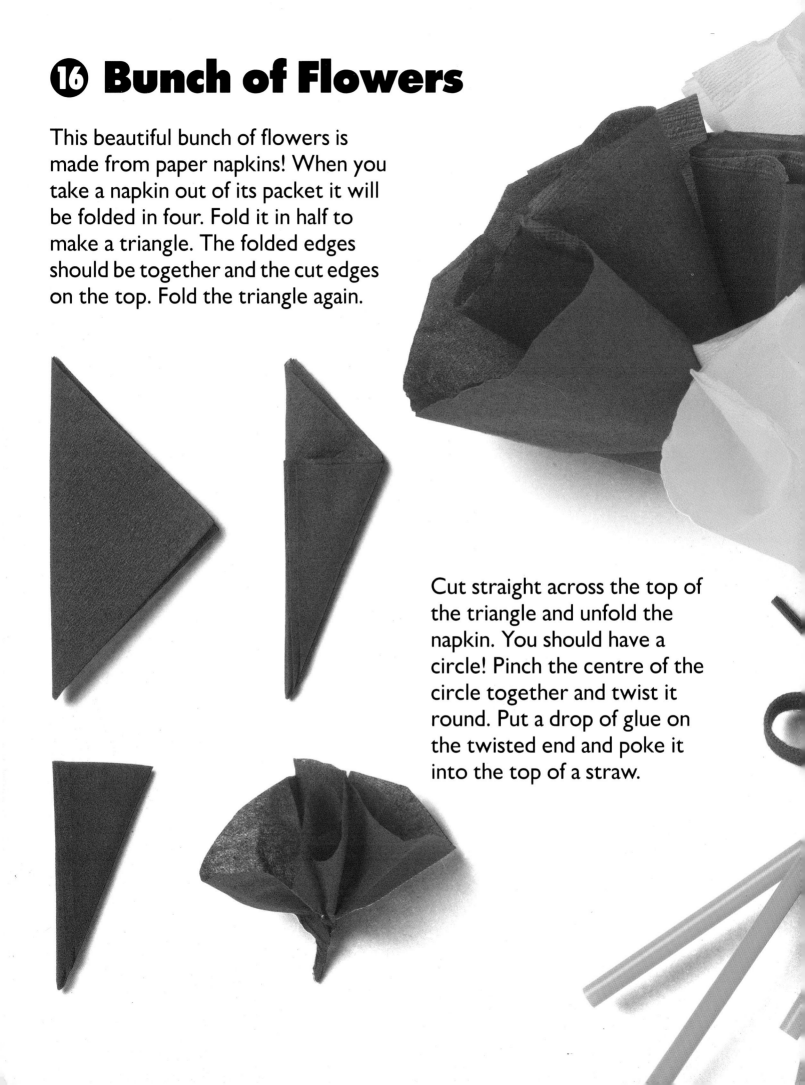

Cut straight across the top of the triangle and unfold the napkin. You should have a circle! Pinch the centre of the circle together and twist it round. Put a drop of glue on the twisted end and poke it into the top of a straw.

Fold and Cut

You can make lots of animals
very easily. Can you remember
how to make concertina folds?

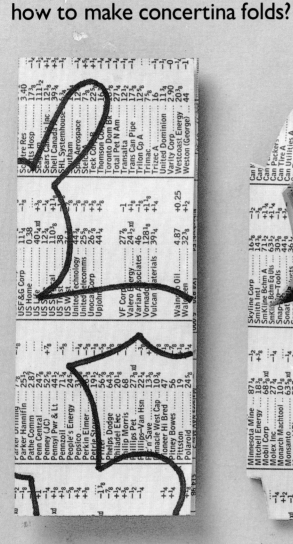

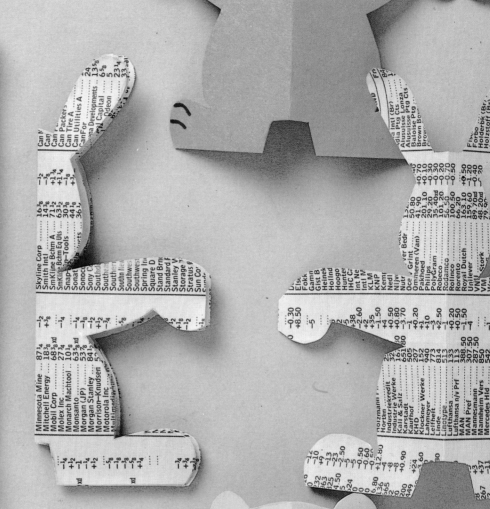

To make rabbits like ours,
concertina fold a strip of thin
paper. Draw the rabbit on the
paper. Make sure that the
middle of its body and the end
of its paw are on folds. Cut the
rabbit out but do not cut
through the folds. Unfold your
chain of rabbits!

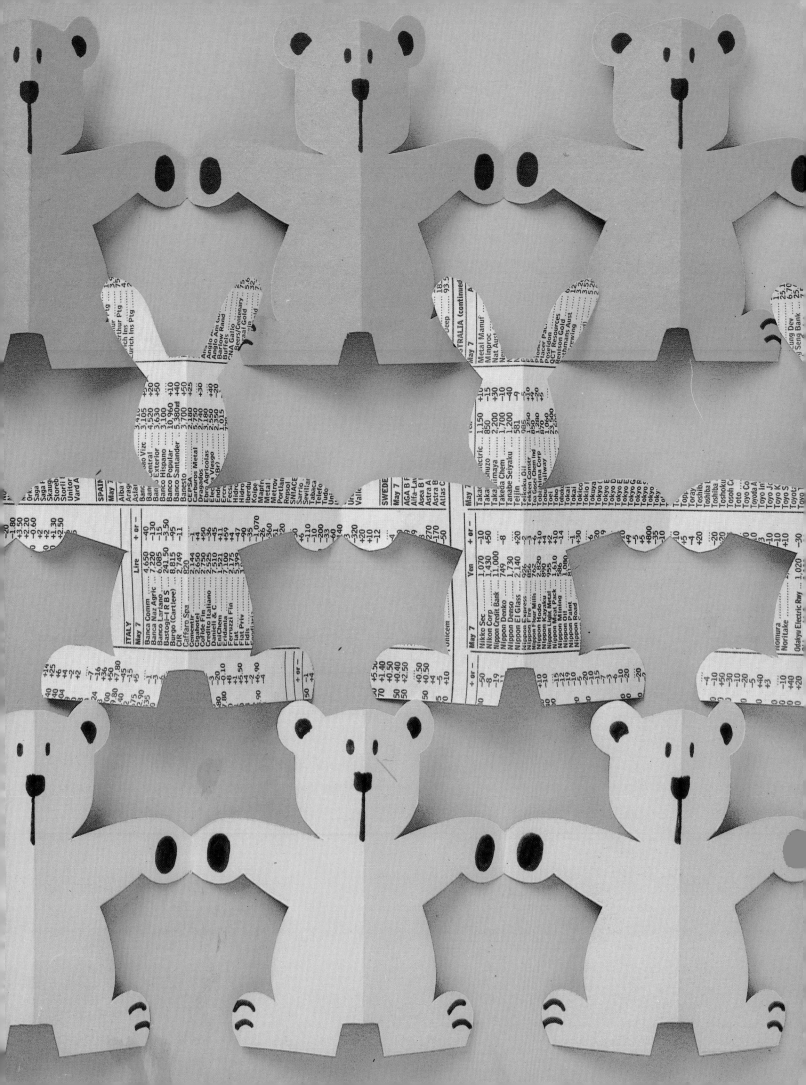

20 Pictures

Here is an easy way for you to make cards for all your friends. First, fold a rectangle of card in half to make the background for your card. Ask a grown-up for two jam jar lids, one bigger than the other.

Put one lid on a square of coloured paper and tear the paper carefully round the outside to make a circle. Do the same with the other lid. What can you make with your circles? Look at the animals and snowman we made!

Here is an idea for making a picture to decorate your room. Collect some coloured paper – even small scraps will be useful. You will also need a piece of fairly stiff paper, or thin card, to make the background for your picture and some glue.

When you have decided what you want your picture to look like, start tearing paper shapes! For our picture, we started with the tree and snake. Can you work out how we made the snake? Next, we added the grass and flowers and then the tiger.

Index

Photographs
By Jon Barnes: 2,3,4,5,10,11,12,13,14,15
By Toby: 6,7,8,9,16,17,18,19,20,21,22,23

First published in Great Britain in 1991 by
Two-Can Publishing Ltd
346 Old Street
London EC1V 9NQ

Copyright © Two-Can Publishing Ltd, 1991

Printed and bound in Hong Kong
2 4 6 8 10 9 7 5 3

British Library Cataloguing in Publication Data
James, Diane
Paint – (Jump! starts craft books)
I. Title   II. Series
649

Pbk ISBN: 1-85434-165-0
Hbk ISBN: 1-85434-108-1